D1665920

# NOWHERE
# TO
# NOW

# NATURE
# POEMS

john david

# THESE NATURE POEMS
## DEDICATED
## TO

MY PARENTS
YOSHIKO
OSHO
PAPAJI
RAMANA MAHARSHI

THESE PEOPLE, AMONGST MANY
OTHERS, HAVE TOUCHED MY LIFE
TO SUCH A PROFOUND DEPTH.
THE JOURNEY WE TOOK TOGETHER
HAS ENRICHED AND NOURISHED
TO SUCH AN EXTENT THEY REMAIN
ALWAYS IN MY HEART.
THEY ARE INSEPERABLE
FROM WHO I AM.
I DEDICATE THIS BOOK TO THEM.


## THANK YOU

# CONTENTS
## MOMENTS ON THE PATH

# Nowhere to Now – Nature Poems

Published by Open Sky Press GbR
office@openskypress.com
www.openskypress.com

First Edition
© Open Sky Press GbR 2023

ISBN: 978-3-943544-77-0

Photographs from the Open Sky House archive.
Cover Drawing by John David.

Printed in Poland

# INTRODUCTION

These poems appeared during a fertile period in my life when I lived in an Indian ashram and was deeply involved in meditation.

I had arrived in the 1980s with society's usual busy mind and soon discovered the virtues of silence which meditation could bring me.

As I became quieter, I noticed that my relationship with nature changed. Shockingly, insects started to appear in my daily life, even though they must have been there before.

It was not only my awareness of insects that increased, I become more conscious of my surroundings. Nature in India is vibrant and lively with many insects, birds and beautiful panoramas.

Completely unexpectedly, fairly long poems started to spontaneously appear in response to my new surroundings. This was in the late 1980s, when I was forty-two. I wrote them down then edited them a little.

Later, inspired by the very short but precise poems I had read from Basho, a Japanese Zen poet, I revisited the longer poems and extracted what seemed to be the essence.

Nine years later, in 1995, I was invited to have an exhibition of my paintings in Bombay, in the Taj Mahal Hotel art gallery. I designed this book and had thirty copies printed, which I sold during the exhibition.

This current incarnation of that little book began in 2020, when I found an old copy and rather liked it.

A young creative resident of Open Sky House, Dhyan, took on the project to find colour photographs that fitted the poems. He did a brilliant job.

Then he left our community and the book was forgotten. Recently I was hunting through my files and again the poems showed up, now with photographs.

Now in October 2023, Om, an inspired graphic designer has done a wonderful job revising the layout of the text, and with Kali, a talented young woman, replacing some photographs and preparing this book for printing.

Being moved yet again by what was created so long ago, I decided to print this new version of the book and offer it to those people I meet who would enjoy it. It touches me that this was a period of my life when I was deeply connected to nature.

It's now clear that humans' belief that they are separate and superior to nature has led us to destroy the natural order, putting humans as a race at risk of our own extinction.

Finally I would say that these HAIKU poems are my response to a period of intense meditation and I offer them to you as a possible focus for your own meditation and spiritual evolution.

John David, October 2023.

# MOMENTS
# ON THE PATH
# 1980 – 1990

# ZEN HAIKU

# MEDITATION
## Introduction

THESE POEMS
WERE
INSPIRED BY
BASHO'S
HAIKU.

EACH HAIKU
HAS BEEN
ABSTRACTED
FROM
A FULL POEM

USE AS A
MANTRA
OR
MEDITATE ON
AS A
KOAN

# CONTENTS
## ZEN HAIKU POEMS

FOGGY LIGHT
DRENCHING

THE
VAST
LANDSCAPE

IN
BEAUTY

SUDDENLY

A BEE

VIVID YELLOW

DIVINE

CROSSES

IN FRONT OF ME

BUFFALO
BELLS

RINGING
OUT

ACROSS

THE VALLEY

WHITE
BUTTERFLIES


DANCE


OVER
THE TREES

DELICATE  LEAVES

FALLING

IN

THE

SUDDEN  BREEZE

DELICIOUS
COOL SILENT
SPRING

A
ROCKY POOL

DEEP
IN THE
PRIMORDIAL FOREST

FERN LEAVES

OPENING
DELICATELY

TOWARDS

THE  SUN

TINY

SHINING  STARS

HANG

IN

THE  TREES

A
SUDDEN
RAINBOW

CAUGHT
ON

THE
SPIDERS
THREAD

IT'S
NICE


WALKING
HOME

IN
THE
RAIN

FROGS

LEAPING

IN

THE
SPRING POND

AS
THE SURF
WASHES BACK

THOUSANDS
OF
SMALL SHELL FISH

SUCK
THEMSELVES
DOWN DEEPER
INTO
THE SAND

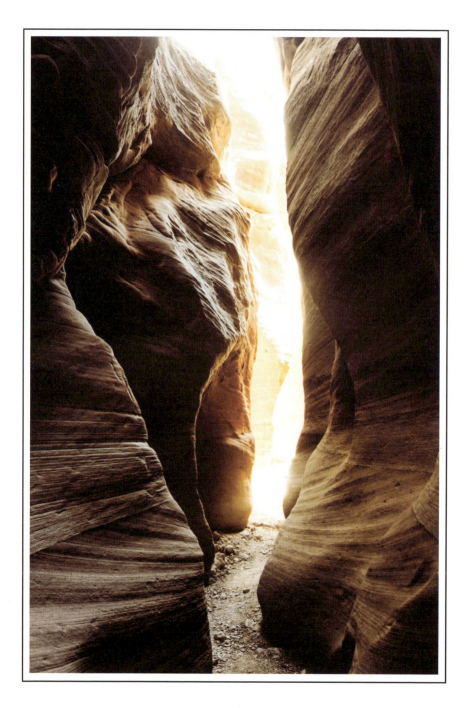

FAR
OFF
SOUNDS

ECHO

THROUGH
MY
HEAD

HUGE HAWKS
SWIRL
UPWARDS

ABOVE
THE  PROMONTORY

INTO
THE  GLARE

OF
THE  SETTING  SUN

THE SMELL

OF
FLOWERS

AND
RICH EARTH

FILL
MY NOSTRILS

SHY

CRABS

AT

SUNSET

TIME

MY
BODY

FEELS
GROUNDED

RESTING
SQUARELY

ON
SUN
BAKED  SOIL

# A

# STEEP

# HILLSIDE

# OF

# CHAOTIC PALMS

HUGE
PUFFY CLOUDS

MOVE
AWAY

TO
INFINITY

THE
SOUND

OF
SINGING  BIRDS

AT

SUNRISE

MAJESTIC
RIVER

FLOWING
ON

AS
BEFORE

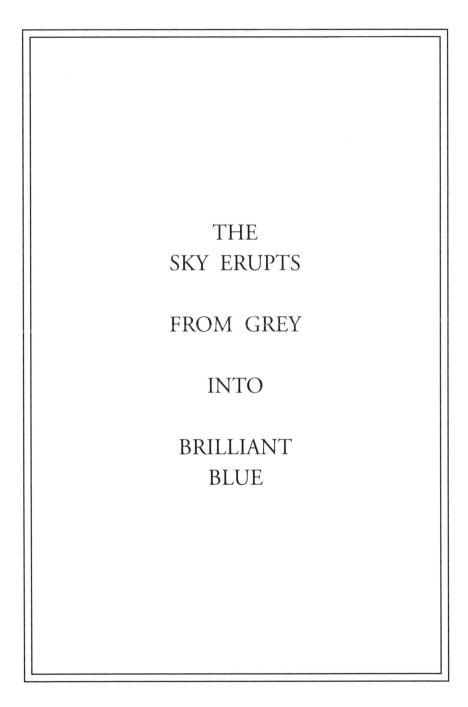

THE
SKY ERUPTS

FROM GREY

INTO

BRILLIANT
BLUE

A

BURST


OF

SUNLIGHT


BUTTERFLIES

ABOUND

THERE IS NO ME

THERE IS NO YOU


THERE IS NO SEPARATION

THERE IS ONLY ONE

THERE IS ONLY LOVE

# MOMENTS
# ON THE PATH
# 1980 – 1990

# NATURE POEMS

# NATURE POEMS
## INTRODUCTION

THESE
POEMS
WERE
WRITTEN
SPONTANEOUSLY
OVER A
PERIOD
OF
EIGHT YEARS

USUALLY
THERE
WAS
A
STIMULUS
AND
A
COMPLETE
POEM
APPEARED

LATER
SOME EDITING

# CONTENTS
## NATURE POEMS

# Sunrise

# Sunrise

SUDDENLY THE SOUND OF
SINGING  BIRDS AT  SUNRISE
PENETRATES  MY  BEING

AWARENESS
OF A  SUBTLE POWER
THE  EARLY  MORNING  SUN

FERN  LEAVES  OPENING  DELICATELY
TOWARDS  THE  SUN

BIRDS  FLEEING  THE  BRANCHES
WINGING  UP  INTO  THE  BLUE

FLOWER  PETALS  LOOSENING
THEIR GRIP
REVEALING  VIBRANT COLOURS

ALL NATURE  REACHING  OUT
TO  THE  COSMIC  VASTNESS

Pune  13th Nov '80

# A Short Walk

# A Short Walk

FROGS LEAPING IN THE SPRING POND
TREES BENDING
TO THE FORCE OF THE WIND
SMOKE HANGING LIKE COTTON
AT THE BOTTOM OF THE VALLEY

HEAT FROM THE STONE PAVEMENT
SEEPING INTO MY SOUL
FOGGY LIGHT DRENCHING
THE VAST LANDSCAPE
IN BEAUTY

RED FLOWERS CLINGING
TO  STALKS DRIED IN THE SUN
BUFFALO BELLS RINGING OUT
ACROSS THE VALLEY
SHADOWS DANCING
ACROSS THE MELTING TARMAC

Panchgani  5<sup>th</sup> Apr '81

# Amongst the Flowers

# Amongst the Flowers

CUTTING FLOWERS
IN THE EARLY MORNING STILLNESS
OF THE GREAT EMPTY VALLEY

STANDING UP
FEELING THE WIND BRUSH SOFTLY
AGAINST MY CHEEK

THE SMELL OF FLOWERS
AND RICH EARTH
FILL MY NOSTRILS

BODY FEELS GROUNDED
RESTING SQUARELY
ON SUN BAKED SOIL

FAR OFF SOUNDS
ECHO THROUGH MY HEAD

FOR JUST A BRIEF MOMENT
MIND STOPS

INTO THIS TOTAL VOID
ENTERS EVERYTHING
AND NOTHING

Rajneeshpuram  18th Apr '86

# Mood Changing

# *Mood Changing*

TINY GREEN BUTTERFLY BUDS
APPEAR SLOWLY
ON THE DRIED UP BUSH
OUTSIDE
THE KITCHEN WINDOW
EACH MORNING A FEW MORE

UNDERSTANDING
TIME PASSING
AND EXISTENCE
CONTINUING
ITS NEVER ENDING CYCLE
SOON WINTER
WILL GIVE WAY TO SPRING

MY
MOODS ALSO CHANGE

London  16th Mar '87

# The River

# The River

MAJESTIC RIVER
FLOWING ON
AS BEFORE

YEARS GONE BY
SAME RIVER

SWIRLING
FLOATING PLANTS
DANCING BACK AND FORTH

WHITE CRANES
STANDING GUARD
OVER A MIRADE OF BIRDS
SINGING
IN HAPHAZARD CONCERT

HUGE PUFFY CLOUDS
MOVE AWAY TO INFINITY

MEMORIES
OF YOUNGER YEARS

Pune  20<sup>th</sup> Apr '87

# Harambol

# I

## Harambol

A TINY FRIENDLY FISHING VILLAGE
AMONGST THE PALMS
TWO GOLDEN PURE SANDY BEACHES

THE FIRST TRANQUIL AND PUBLIC
STREWN WITH FISHING BOATS
THE OTHER ENCLOSED WITH A
FRESHWATER LAKE
AND STRONG ROCKY WAVES

BETWEEN THE TWO
A DIVINE PATHWAY
LINKS THE PLAYGROUNDS

A ROCKY PROMONTORY
A STEEP HILLSIDE OF
CHAOTIC PALMS

BEYOND A JUNGLE
LEADS TO
A SILENT BANYAN TREE

# II

## Harambol

HERE IN GOA
A PARADISE
IN PHYSICAL FORM

A PLACE
TO BE IN NATURE
MELTING AND ALONE

OF ONENESS
AND
BLISSFULNESS

THANK YOU
FOR BRINGING ME
TO SUCH A PLACE
WITHIN MYSELF


Goa - Harambol  16th May '87

# Nature's Silence

# I

## Nature's Silence

SHY CRABS
AT SUNSET TIME
PERCHED ON THE EDGE
OF THEIR SAND HOLES

CONVOYS OF ANTS
LARGE AND SMALL
DETERMINEDLY
MOVING SOME HUGE LOAD

LIZARDS
SCURRYING  AROUND
THE WALL LAMP
STOPPING AND TAKING A PUZZLED
LOOK AROUND


UNEXPECTEDLY
BLACK SCORPION
HURRYING ACROSS THE FIREPLACE
AS FRIGHTENED AS I


HORIZONTALLY STRIPED FISH
DARTING AROUND ME
IN THE LAKE
TAKING SUDDEN SHARP BITES

# II

## Nature's Silence

FLIES ALWAYS
BUZZ AROUND
TICKLING AT THOSE MOST
PROFOUND MOMENTS OF SILENCE

HUGE HAWKS
SWIRL UPWARDS
ABOVE THE PROMONTORY
INTO THE GLARE
OF THE SETTING SUN

A KINGFISHER
BRILLIANT BLUE
SITTING ON A ROCK IN THE LAKE
DARTS DOWN SUDDENLY

AS THE SURF
WASHES BACK
THOUSANDS
OF SMALL SHELL FISH
SUCK THEMSELVES DOWN
DEEPER INTO THE SAND

ALL THIS
COMES OUT OF
MY OWN DEPTH OF
SILENCE AND STILLNESS

Goa - Harambol  28th May '87

# Monsoon

# Monsoon

## THE
## MONSOON
## COMES

PLANTS
BURST
FORTH

BUTTERFLIES
DANCE BY

WHAT DELIGHT

Goa  31st May '87

# White Butterflies

# White Butterflies

THIS MORNING
EATING BREAKFAST

MANY WHITE BUTTERFLIES
DANCE OVER THE TREES

AS IF TO SAY
CELEBRATE WITH PLAY

I RETURN HAPPILY
TO MY FLOWER PAINTING

Laxmi Villas, Pune  4th Aug '87

# Birds

# Birds

IT'S DAYBREAK
THE BIRDS ARE SINGING
EXCITEDLY  WELCOMING
THE DAWN OF A NEW DAY

NOT FOR THEM
THE MEMORY OF YESTERDAY
NOR
THE EXPECTATION OF TOMORROW

THEIR
LITTLE BEINGS
ARE TUNED ONLY
TO CELEBRATE NOW

Laxmi Villas, Pune  17th Aug '87

# A Burst
# of
# Sunlight

# A Burst of Sunlight

MONSOON
IS OVER

A BURST
OF SUNLIGHT

BUTTERFLIES
ABOUND

A BRIGHTER
PARADISE

Laxmi Villas, Pune  13th Sept '87

# Walking in the Rain

# Walking in the Rain

WALKING HOME
IN THE RAIN TONIGHT
I FIND HOW NICE IT IS

STRANGELY
A NEW KIND OF WETNESS
DIFFERENT FROM DRYNESS
BUT NOT AS WET AS I REMEMBER

FINDING THAT RAIN
IS MERELY
DIFFERENT FROM DRYNESS

HOW NICE IT IS
WALKING HOME
IN THE RAIN

Pune  2nd Oct '87

# Shining Stars

# Shining Stars

## THIS MORNING

AS THE RAIN
STOPS

THE SUN
COMES OUT

TINY SHINING
STARS

HANG
IN THE TREES

Laxmi Villas, Pune  6th Oct '87

# Birds and Silence

# Birds and Silence

A MOMENT
OF DEEP SILENCE
ALONE
IN MY ROCKING CHAIR

SUDDENLY
A GREEN PARROT
CHATTERING
AROUND THE TOWER

THREE NEW BIRDS
HOPPING
TOGETHER IN THE TALLEST TREE

A TINY HUMMING BIRD
DRINKING FROM A LEAF

FEELING
SO DEEPLY HERE
IN THIS SILENT MOMENT

BLISS

Laxmi Villas, Pune  22nd Oct '87

# In the Garden

# In the Garden

SITTING
ON THE CONCRETE BENCH

MELTING
GRADUALLY INTO THE GARDEN

THE BRIGHT YELLOW
GREEN PALM LEAF

A WHITE AND BLACK BIRD
HOPPING

A SUDDEN RAINBOW
CAUGHT ON THE SPIDER'S THREAD

A SPRINKLING
OF BUTTERFLIES

DELICATE LEAVES
FALLING
IN THE SUDDEN BREEZE

AN OPENING IN MY HEART

Laxmi Villas, Pune 26th Nov '87

# Brilliant
# Red Tree

# Brilliant Red Tree

LOOKING OUT
AT THE TREE
I KNOW AS GREEN

I SEE IT COVERED
WITH AN ABUNDANCE
OF RED FLOWERS

SMALL BIRDS
HANG UPSIDE DOWN
DRINKING FROM THE LEAVES

A MULTITUDE
OF GORGEOUS BUTTERFLIES
DANCE
OVER THE FLOWERS

A CHIPMUNK
CLIMBS PRECARIOUSLY
ALONG THE BRANCHES
FEASTING ON SEED

Pune  25th Feb '88

# The Rainy Season

# The Rainy Season

THE LONG
DAMP COLD
RAINY SEASON
FINALLY
COME TO AN END

THE LUSH
GREEN GARDEN
WELCOMES
MULTITUDES
OF DANCING BUTTERFLIES

THE SKY
ERUPTS FROM
GREY INTO BRILLIANT BLUE
YELLOW FLOWERS
CASCADE ALL OVER

A PAIR
OF HUGE
GREEN ELEGANT
GOD BIRDS
SING MADLY TO EACH OTHER

Laxmi Villas, Pune  25th Oct '88

Love is

# Love is

LOVE IS
ONLY LOVE IS
LOVE MOVES THE LEAVES IN THE WIND
AND THE PLANETS IN THE UNIVERSE
ALL IS LOVE AND YOU ARE THIS LOVE

AUTHENTIC LOVE IS BEYOND NAMES
AND FORMS
CONSTANTLY THERE
EVER EXPANDING
EVER FLOWING SOURCE OF ALL
EVERYTHING RISES FROM THIS LOVE
AND YOU ARE THIS LOVE

AUTHENTIC LOVE KNOWS
THERE IS NO ME
THERE IS NO YOU
THERE IS NO SEPARATION
THERE IS ONLY ONE
THERE IS ONLY LOVE

THERE IS ONLY LOVE
LOVE SIMPLY IS.

Laxmi Villas, Pune  25th Oct '88

# AUTO BIOGRAPHY

I was born in Wales, UK, on December 8th 1944 to a Family Psychiatrist father and a housewife mother. My mother was a lovely looking, heartful woman, who cared for me and my brothers Richard and Roger, and my sister Cheryll.

While my mother encouraged us to play, my father studied and wrote many books on psychiatry and later excellent gardening books on Clementis and Roses. Touchingly, after he had retired, he bought a Hasselblad camera and took all his own flower photos from his extensive garden to illustrate his books.

I attended university where I studied Civil Engineering and after about six years working in a famous London design office returned as a mature student to study Architecture.

At this time my life could be seen as successful on the outside, but gradually through my twenties I had become dissatisfied with my inner world. My initial step towards a different experience was to work in Tokyo, first as an architect then as an English teacher. Here I met Yoshiko, a quiet and heartful clothes designer. We later married, travelling to India to stay at Osho's Ashram in Pune.

In this Ashram I developed a lifelong meditation practice, which gradually brought my inner world into harmony. Osho's talks stimulated my interest in the great historic Spiritual Masters. Later I visited H. W. L. Poonjaji (Papaji) in whose presence I realised the truth of my own being. It was during those years that I got to know Sri Ramana Maharshi, a modern Indian Saint.

After spending some twelve years living in India I returned to the West. To Australia in fact, where I lived for six years and met my second wife, Sally. On my way back to Europe I spent a year in a personal retreat at Arunachala, a mountain in south India considered to be the Heart chakra of our planet and where Ramana Maharshi spent most of his life.

Later I returned to Europe, to Germany, where I have now lived for twenty-three years. I found myself sharing the spiritual knowledge I had gained, intensely travelling throughout Europe holding evening meetings and weekend intensives.

A community of roughly twenty people has grown around me spontaneously since 2002. It grew from my first summer retreat taking place on a horse farm in the Black Forest. Later we moved to our present location in Hitdorf, directly on the bank of the Rhine between Cologne and Düsseldorf, a huge historic mansion built in 1666: Open Sky House.

In the last years a community has developed outside Kyiv, Ukraine, comprising a seminar centre and small hotel. As well, after renting for five years, our landlord in Spain has provided a loan that has allowed us to buy our Villa in a very beautiful and quiet part of Denia, near Valencia just minutes from the Mediterranean.

I would consider myself a multifaceted creative person. I like to paint and photograph and in recent years used my architectural skills to develop our centre near Kyiv and our Spanish house. I've also very much enjoyed writing ten spiritual books and directing six Spiritual films.

I make myself available to meet anybody who finds me and wishes to know themselves. I hold regular meetings through the internet and hold regularly retreats including twenty-two years at Arunachala Mountain in South India each January.

At my advanced age (78) I have two daughters, seven-year-old twins Naomi and Amelia, with, a former young partner, Yulia. Now separated, we parent the girls together and they are becoming my final teachers; tremendous characters and a huge joy who enliven all they come in close contact with.

Finally, a huge gratitude to existence for the wonderful unfolding of my life's destiny.

# Spiritual Books
## by John David

**Arunachala Talks**
English and German
**Arunachala Shiva**
English, German, Russian
**Papaji Amazing Grace**
English and German
**The Pointless Joy of Freedom**
English, German, Russian
**The Great Misunderstanding**
English, German, Russian, Spanish
**Meetings with Remarkable People**
English, German, Spanish
**Blueprints for Awakening – European Masters**
English and German
**Blueprints for Awakening – Indian Masters**
English, German, Russian
**Aham Sphurana – A Glimpse of Self Realisation**
English, German, Spanish, Tamil
**Papaji – Day by Day**
English, German, Spanish

# Films by John David
## with subtitles in many languages

**Satori Moments with Vijaya**

**The Great Misunderstanding**

**The Pointless Joy of Freedom**

**Satori**
**Metamorphosis of an Awakening**

**Blueprints for Awakening**
**Indian Masters**

**Arunachala Shiva**
**Commentaries on 'Who Am I?'**

**Blueprints for Awakening**
**European Spiritual Masters**

www.johndavid.international